GRACE WILLIAMS

# FANTASIA
## ON
## WELSH NURSERY TUNES

SCORE

Music Department
OXFORD UNIVERSITY PRESS
Oxford and New York

*Oxford University Press, Great Clarendon Street, Oxford OX2 6DP, England*
*Oxford University Press Inc., 198 Madison Avenue, New York, NY 10016, USA*

*Oxford is a trade mark of Oxford University Press*

## *Orchestration*

2 Flutes
(2nd doubling Piccolo)
2 Oboes
2 Clarinets (B♭ and A)
2 Bassoons
2 Horns
2 Trumpets
3 Trombones

Timpani (one player)
Percussion (two players):
Side Drum
Cymbals
Tambourine
Triangle
Glockenspiel
Harp
Strings

The following instruments may be omitted:-
2nd Oboe, 2nd Bassoon, 3rd and 4th Horns.
These are cued in other players' parts.

The Percussion may be reduced to either one timpanist and one percussion player or one player for timpani and percussion. A condensed percussion part is provided for this purpose.

Duration: 10½ minutes

The score is a facsimile of the composer's manuscript.

This work has been recorded by the Royal Philharmonic Orchestra conducted by Sir Charles Groves on Lyrita SRCD323.

# FANTASIA ON WELSH NURSERY TUNES

GRACE WILLIAMS

Printed in Great Britain
OXFORD UNIVERSITY PRESS, MUSIC DEPARTMENT, GREAT CLARENDON STREET, OXFORD OX2 6DP

Flts.
Obs.
Clts. A
Bsns.
Hns. F
Trpts. Bb
Trbns.
Timp.
S.D.
Glock.
Harp
Vlns. 1
Vlns. 2
Vlas.
'Cellos
Bass.
mf
f
mp

10
Flts.
Obs.
Clts. A
Bsns.
Hns. F
Tpts. Bb
Solo
Trbns.
Timp.
S. D.
Glock.
Harp
Vlns. 1
Vlns. 2
Vlas.
'Cellos
Bas.
mf
f
mp
f con amore
(nondiv.)
f con amore
f con amore
Pizz
f con amore

A
Flts.
Obs.
Clts. A
Solo
f
Bsns.
1
2
Hns. F
3
4
Trpts. Bb
1
2
Trbns.
3
Timp.
Triangle
mf
Perc.
Harp
f
ff
f
A
Vlns. 1
Vlns. 2
div.
Vlas
f
unis.
'Cellos
Bass

20
Flts.
Obs.
mf
Clts.
Bsns.
mf
1
2
con sord.
mf
Hns. F
3
4
Trpts. Bb
1
2
Trbns.
3
Timp.
Perc.
Tambourine
mp
mf
Harp
Vlns. 1
mf
Vlns. 2
mf
Vlas.
mf
'Cellos
mf
Bass.
mf

Poco rit . . . . . . . a tempo
Flts.
Obs.
solo
mf dolce
Clts. A
ff
mp dolce
Bsns.
ff
mp dolce
Hns. F
1 2
3 4
Senza sord.
f
Trpts. Bb
f
Trbns.
1 2
3
Timp.
Triangle
mp
Tamb.
f
Harp
poco rit . . . . . . a tempo
Vlns. 1
f
fp
f
ff
mp dolce
Vlns. 2
f
fp
f
ff
mf dolce
Vlas.
f
mf
f
ff
mp dolce
'Cellos
fp
f
ff
mp dolce
Bass.
f
f
mp

B
Flts.
mf scherzoso
Obs.
mf scherzoso
Clts. A
Bsns.
mf scherzoso
Hns. F
1
2
3
4
Trpts. Bb
con sord.
Solo
mf scherzoso
Trbns.
1
2
3
Timp.
Triangle
Glock.
mf scherzoso
Harp
B
Vlns. 1
Pizz.
mf scherzoso
Vlns. 2
mp
Pizz.
mf scherzoso
Vlas.
mf scherzoso
'Cellos
Pizz.
mf scherzoso
Bass.

30
Poco rit. . . . . . . . .
Flts.
Obs.
solo
mf
f
Clts. A
mf
Bsns.
mf
1
2
Hns. F
3
4
(con sord.)
mf
Trpts. Bb
mf
mf
1
2
Trbns.
3
Timp.
Trg.
Glock.
Harp
Poco rit. . . . .
Vlns. 1
f
Vlns. 2
f
Vlas.
mf
'Cellos
f
Bass.

a tempo
35
Flts.
Obs.
mf
Clts.
mp
Bsns.
mp
1
2
Hns. F
3
4
mp
Tpts. Bb
mp
1
2
Trbns.
3
Timp.
S.D.
Glock.
mp
Harp
mp
a tempo
Vlns. 1
mp
arco
pp
Vlns. 2
mp
arco
pp
Vlas.
Pizz.
mp
arco
pp
'Cellos
Pizz.
mp
arco
pp
Bass.
[Pizz.]
mp

C
40
Flts.
solo
Obs.
mf dolce
ff deciso
Clts. A
ff deciso
Bsns.
ff deciso
Hns. F
1
2
3
4
Trpts. Bb
(Consord.)
ff deciso
Tbns.
1
2
3
Timp.
mf deciso
S.D.
Glock.
Harp
mf
C
Vlns. 1
P sub.
mf espress.
Vlns. 2
P sub.
mp
espress.
mf
Vlas.
div.
unis.
P sub.
espress.
mf
Cellos
P sub.
espress.
mf
Bass.
arco
p
espress.
mf

Flts.
Obs.
Clts. A
to Clts. in B♭
Bsns.
Hns. F
senza sord.
ritmico
Tripts. B♭
Trbns.
Timp
S.D.
Cymbals
Harp
Vlns. 1
Vlns. 2
Vlas.
'Cellos
Bass.
Pizz.
mf dolce
ff ritmico

45

Piccolo
Fl. 1
Obs.
Clts. Bb
Bsns.
Hns. F
Trpts. Bb
senza sord.
ritmico
Trbns.
Timp.
tr.
S.D.
Cymb.
cl.
Harp
Vlns. 1
ritmico
Vlns. 2
ritmico
Vlas.
Cellos
Pizz.
Bass.

50
Picc.
Fl. 1
Obs.
Clts. Bb
Bsns.
Hns. F
Trpts. Bb
Trbns.
Timp.
S.D.
Glock.
Harp
Vlns. 1
Vlns. 2
Vlas.
Pizz.
'Cellos
Bass.

D
Picc.
Fl. 1
Obs.
Clts. Bb
Bsns.
a2
Hns. F
Trpts. Bb
Trbns.
Timp.
(Tamb.)
Tambourine
Glock.
Harp
D
Vlns. 1
Vlns. 2
Vlas.
'Cellos
Bass.
nut
arco
(Pizz)

rit. . . . . . . . . .
Picc.
Fl. 1
Obs.
Solo
Clts. Bb
Bsns.
Hns. F
Trpts. Bb
Trbns.
Timp.
Tamb.
Glock.
Harp
nut
rit. . . . . .
Vlns. 1
Vlns. 2
Vlas.
'Cellos
arco
Bass.

a tempo
E
to Fl 2
a2
Picc.
Fl. 1
Obs.
Clts. Bb
Bsns.
Hns. F
Trpts. Bb
Trbns.
Timp.
Tamb.
Glock.
Harp
a tempo
nut
div.
sim.
pizz.
Vlns. 1
Vlns. 2
Vlas.
'Cellos
Bass.

Flts.
Obs.
Clts. Bb
Bsns.
Hns.
Trpts. Bb
Trbns.
Timp
Tamb.
Glock.
Harp
Vlns. 1
Vlns. 2
Vlas.
'Cellos
Bass.
sim.
(nondiv.)

rit.
a tempo
Flts.
a2
Obs.
a2
Clts. Bb
Bsns.
a2
Hns F
1
2
3
4
Trpts. Bb
a2
Trbs.
1
2
3
Timp.
Triangle
Glock.
Harp
rit.
a tempo
Vlns. 1
Vlns. 2
div.
unis.
Vlas.
'Cellos
Bass.
arco
Pizz.

Flts.
a2
Obs.
a2
Clts. Bb
a2
Bsns.
Hns. F
mf
Trpts. Bb
Trbns.
Timp.
Triangle
cymb.
Harp
Vlns. 1
Vlns. 2
Vlas
div.
non div.
'Cellos
div.
non div.
Bass.

link
80
Flts.
Obs.
Clts. Bb
Bsns.
Hns. F
Trpts. Bb
Trbns.
Timp.
Triangle
Cymb.
Harp
Vlns. 1
Vlns. 2
Vlas.
'Cellos
Bass.
molto cantando
molto cantando
Pizz
arco
arco
mp molto cantando

Poco rit. . . . .
Flts.
Obs.
solo
Clts.Bb
Solo
mf
Bsns.
Hns.F
1 2
3 4
Trpts.Bb
Trbns.
1 2
3
Timp
Tri.
Cymb.
Harp
poco rit. . . . .
Vlns 1
mf
molto cantando
Vlns. 2
mf
Vlas.
'Cellos
div.
Bass.

F
a tempo 𝅗𝅥 = 100
Flts.
Solo
mf molto tranquillo
Obs.
Clts. Bb
mp dolce
mp
Bsns.
p dolce
p
Hns. 1 2 3 4
Trpts. Bb
Trbns. 1 2 3
Timp.
Tri.
Cymb.
Harp
F
a tempo 𝅗𝅥 = 100
Vlns. 1
p
pp tranquillo
Vlns. 2
p
pp tranquillo
Vlas.
p
pp tranquillo
'Cellos
unis.
p
pp tranquillo
Bass.
p
pp

90
Flts.
Obs.
Clts. Bb
Bsns.
Vlns. 1
Vlns. 2
Vlas.
'Cellos
Bass.
Flts.
Obs.
Clts Bb
Bsns.
Vlns. 1
Vlns. 2
Vlas
'Cellos
Bass.

Flts.
Obs.
Clts. Bb
Bsns.
Vlns. 1
Vlns. 2
Vlas.
'Cellos
Bass.
100
Flts.
Obs.
Clts. Bb
Bsns.
Vlns. 1
Vlns. 2
Vlas.
'Cellos
Bass.

Flts.
Obs.
Clts Bb
Bsns.
Vlns. 1
Vlns. 2
Vlas.
'Cellos
Bass.
div.
div.
pp
tranquillo
Flts.
Obs.
Clts. Bb
Bsns.
Vlns. 1
Vlns. 2
Vlas.
'Cellos
Bass.
unis.
unis.

G
animando
Flts.
Obs.
Clts. Bb
Bsns.
con sord.
Hns. F
animando
con sord.
Tpts. Bb
con sord.
con sord.
Tbns.
Timp.
Triangle
Cymb.
Harp
G
animando
Vlns. 1
Vlns. 2
Vlas.
Cellos
Bass.

Flts.
Obs.
Clts. Bb
Bsns.
Hns. F
Trpts. Bb
Trbns.
Timp.
Tri.
Cymb.
soft dr. st.
Harp
Vlns. 1
Vlns. 2
Vlas.
Cellos
Bass.

120

rit. . . . molto rit. .
a2
Flts.
Obs.
Clts. B♭
Bsns.
Hns. F
Trpts. B♭
Tbns.
Timp.
rit. . . . molto rit. .
Tri.
Cymb.
tr
Harp
rit. . . . molto rit. .
Vlns. 1
Vlns. 2
Vlas.
Cellos
div.
Bass.

a tempo
Flts.
a2
Obs.
Clts. Bb
Bsns.
Hns. F
Tpts. Bb
Trbns.
Timp.
a tempo
Tri.
Cymb.
Harp
a tempo
div.
unis.
Vlns. 1
Vlns. 2
Vlas.
'Cellos
Bass.

Poco rall . . . . . .
Flts.
mf dolce
Obs.
mf
dolce
Clts Bb
mp
dolce
dim . . .
Bsns.
mf dolce
mp
dim . . . . . . .
Hns F
1
2
3
4
mp dolce
dim. poco a poco
Tpts. Bb
mp dolce
dim. poco a poco
Tbns.
1
2
3
mp dolce
dim. poco a poco
pp
Timp.
Poco rall . . . .
Tri.
mf
mp
S.D
Harp
mf dolce
dim. poco a poco
Poco rall . . .
Vlns. 1
mf dolce
dim. poco a poco
Vlns. 2
mf
mf dolce
dim. poco a poco
Vlas.
div.
non div.
mf dolce
dim. poco a poco
'Cellos
div.
mf dolce
dim. poco a poco
Bass
mf
dim. poco a poco

S 129

H
a tempo 𝅗𝅥=120
canon
Flts
Obs.
Solo
mp
scherzoso
Clts. Bb
to Clts. in A
pp
Bsns.
pp
Solo
scherzoso
Hns. F
senza sord.
mf
mp
p
Tpts. Bb
Tbns.
Timp.
Tri.
S. D.
p
Harp
p
H
a tempo 𝅗𝅥=120
Vlns. 1
p
pp
Vlns. 2
p
pp
Vlas.
Pizz
arco
pp
Cellos
Pizz
p
Bass
Pizz
p

140
Flts.
mp
scherzoso
Obs.
mp
scherzoso
a2
Clts. A
mp
scherzoso
Bsns.
Hns. F
Tpts. Bb
Tbns.
Timp.
Tri.
pp
S.D.
Harp
Vlns. 1
Pizz
Vlns. 2
Pizz.
Vlas.
Pizz.
'Cellos
div.
pp
Bass.
pp

Flts.
(mp)
Obs.
(mp)
mf
Clts. A
(mp)
Bsns.
Solo – (senza sord.)
mf
Hns. F
1
2
3
4
(con sord.)
mf
Trpts. Bb
Trbns.
1
2
3
Timp.
Tri.
S.D.
Harp
Vlns. 1
p
mp
p
Vlns. 2
p
mp
p
Vlas.
p
mp
p
Cellos
div.
p
mp
p
Bass.
p
mp
p

150

I
Flts.
mf
Obs.
Clts. A
Bsns.
mf
Hns. F
Trpts. Bb
mf
Solo
Trbns.
Timp.
Tri.
S.D.
mp
Harp
I
Vlns. 1
Vlns. 2
Vlas.
'Cellos
nondiv.
Bass.

Flts.
Obs.
Soli
Clts. A
Bsns.
Hns. F
Trpts. Bb
Trbns.
Timp.
Tri.
Glock.
Harp
Vlns. 1
arco
cantabile
Vlns. 2
Vlas.
Cellos
arco
(mp)
Bass.
arco
mf
mp
p
pp

160
6
rall - - - -
J
Poco meno mosso
♩=88
Obs.
soli
mp
dolce
Bsns.
pp
Trpts. Bb
Poco meno mosso
Triangle
rall - - - -
Vlns. 1
Vlns. 2
arco
Vlas.
'Cellos
div. Pizz
Bass.
Pizz
170
Obs.
Bsns.
Tri.
Vlns. 1
Vlns. 2
Vlas.
'Cellos
Bass.

K
Flts
Obs.
Clts. A
Bsns.
Hns. F
Trpts. Bb
Trbns.
Timp.
Tri.
Glock.
Harp
Vlns. 1
Vlns. 2
Vlas.
Cellos
Bass.
mp
mf
[con sord.]
con amore
arco

180
Flts.
mp
Obs.
mp
Clts. A
mp
Bsns.
mp
Hns. F
Trpts. Bb
mp
Trbns.
mp
Timp.
Tri.
Glock.
Harp
Vlns. 1
mp
Vlns. 2
mp
Vlas.
mp
'Cellos
mp
Bass.
mp

Flts.
Obs.
Clts.
Bsns.
Hns F
Trpts. Bb
Solo
mf
Trbns.
Timp.
Tri.
Glock.
Harp
Vlns. 1
pp sotto voce
Vlns. 2
pp sotto voce
Vlas.
pp sotto voce
'Cellos
pp sotto voce
Bass.
pp sotto voce

190

stringendo
L
Tempo Primo 𝅗𝅥 = 152
Flts.
a2
Obs
Solo
mp
a2
Clts. A
Bsns.
Hns. F.
senza sord.
Tripts. B♭
senza sord.
a2
con fuoco
Trbns.
senza sord.
a2
con fuoco
Timp.
Tri.
Glock.
Harp
stringendo
L
Tempo Primo
𝅗𝅥 = 152
Vlns. 1
Pizz.
Vlns. 2
Pizz.
Vlas.
Pizz.
'Cellos
Pizz.
Bass.
Pizz.

Flts.
a2
ff
Obs.
a2
ff
Clts. A
a2
ff
Bsns.
a2
ff
Hns F.
1
2
3
4
Trpts. Bb
Trbns.
1
2
3
Timp.
f
Tri.
f
Glock.
Harp
ff
Vlns. 1
arco
cantando
Vlns. 2
arco
con fuoco
f
div.
f
cantando
non div.
Vlas.
arco
con fuoco
div.
f
cantando
'Cellos
arco
con fuoco
f
cantando
Bass.
con fuoco
arco
Pizz.
con fuoco
f
cantando

200
Flts.
Obs.
Clts. A
Bsns.
Hns. F
Tpts. Bb
Trbns.
Timp.
Cymb.
soft st.
Glock.
Harp
Vlns. 1
Vlns. 2
div.
Vlas.
unis.
'Cellos
Bass.

poco rit . . . . . . a tempo
Flts.
a2
Obs.
Clts. A
Soli
Bsns.
Hns. F
Tpts. B♭
Tbns.
senza sord.
Timp.
tr
Cymb.
mp
Glock.
Harp
poco rit . . . . . atempo
Vlns. 1
Vlns. 2
unis.
Vlas.
'Cellos
Bass.
arco

M
Flts.
ff gioeoso
a2
Obs.
ff
gioeoso
Clts. A
gioeoso
a2
Bsns.
f
ff gioeoso
1
2
Hns.F
3
4
Soli
Tripts Bb
mf
f
gioeoso
1
2
Tbns.
mf
f
gioeoso
3
f
gioeoso
Timp.
f
el.
Cymb.
f
Gloek.
Harp
M
gioeoso
Vlns. 1
f
ff
Vlns. 2
ff
gioeoso
Pizz.
Vlas.
f
ff
giocoso
Pizz.
'Cellos
f
gioeoso
ff
Pizz.
Bass.
f
ff
gioeoso

210

Flts.
Obs.
Solo
mf
mp
a2
Clts. A
f
mf
Bsns.
Hns. F
1
2
3
4
Trpts. Bb
mf
Soli
a2
mp
Trbns.
1
2
3
mf
Timp.
mf
Cymb.
mf
Glock.
p
Harp
Pizz.
Vlns. 1
f
mf
p
Vlns. 2
f
mf
Pizz.
p
Vlas.
arco.
f
mf
Pizz.
p
'Cellos
f
mf
div.
p
Bass.
f
p

T
Meno mosso [Alla marcia]
rit. . .
Flts.
Obs.
Clts. A
Bsns.
Hns. F
Trpts. Bb
(a2)
ff declamando
Trbns.
Timp
Cymb.
S.D.
Harp
ff
mp
Meno Mosso [Alla marcia]
rit. . . .
declamando
arco
Vlns. 1
Vlns. 2
Vlas.
'Cellos
Bass.
mp sub.
div. arco

N Andante con moto ♩=88
220
Flts.
Obs.
Clts. A
Bsns.
Hns. F
Vlns. 1
Vlns. 2
Vlas.
'Cellos
Bass.
a2
molto espress.
molto espress. e legato
soli
div.
unis.
Obs.
Vlns. 1
Vlns. 2
Vlas.
'Cellos
Bass

O
Flts.
Obs.
Clts. A
Bsns.
Hns. F
Tpts. Bb
Trbns.
Timp.
Tri.
S.D.
Harp
Vlns. 1
Vlns. 2
Vlas.
'Cellos
Bass.
mf
con amore
a2
pp
unis.
pizz.
div.
mp

poco ten... a tempo
Flts.
Obs.
Clts. A
Bsns.
Hns.
Trpts. Bb
Trbns.
Timp
Tri.
S.D.
Harp
poco ten... a tempo
Vlns. 1
Vlns. 2
Vlas.
'Cellos
Bass.
unis.

Flts.
dolce
Obs.
dolce
Clts. A
dolce
Bsns.
dolce
Hns. F
Trpts. Bb
Trbns.
Timp.
Tri.
S.D.
Harp
dolce
Vlns. 1
dolce
Vlns. 2
dolce
molto legato
Vlas.
dolce
'Cellos
dolce
Pizz
arco div.
Bass.
dolce
arco

240

Flts
Obs.
Clts. A
Bsns.
Vlns 1
Vlns. 2
Vlas.
Cellos
Bass.
mp
legato
div.
mf
soli
mf legato
Flts.
Obs.
Clts. A
Bsns.
Vlns 1
Vlns. 2
Vlas.
Cellos
Bass.
p

P
Obs.
dolce
Bsns.
p dolce
Harp
p dolce
mp
Vlns. 1
Vlns. 2
Pizz
arco
Vlas.
div.
'Cellos
arco div.
Bass.
250
Clts. A
consord.
Trpts. Bb
Vlns. 1
Vlns. 2
unis.
Sul D
Vlas.
'Cellos
Bass.

Poco rit . . . . . . . . a tempo 𝅗𝅥 = 96
Obs.
Solo
mp
dolce
Clts. A
Bsns.
p dolce
Tpts. Bb
3
Poco rit . . . . . . . a tempo
Vlns. 1
Vlns. 2
p
pp
Vlas.
pp
'Cellos
p
pp
Bass.
poco più mosso . . . .
Flts.
Solo
mp
Obs.
Clts. A
Solo
mp
Bsns.
poco più mosso . . . .
Vlns. 1
pp
subito
Vlns. 2
pp
subito
Vlas.
pp
subito
'Cellos
subito
Bass.
pp
subito

Q Tempo Primo ♩=152
Flts.
Obs.
Clts. A
Bsns.
Hns. F
Trpts. Bb
senza sord.
deciso
Tbns.
Timp.
Tri.
S.D.
Harp
Q Tempo Primo ♩=152
Vlns. 1
deciso
Vlns. 2
Pizz.
deciso
Vlas.
Cellos
Bass.

Flts.
Obs.
Clts. A
Bsns.
Hns. F
Tpts. Bb
Tbns.
Timp.
Tri
S.D.
Harp
Vlns. 1
Vlns. 2
Vlas.
'Cellos
Bass.
ff
tr

Flts.
a2
Obs.
a2
Clts. A
a2
ff
Bsns.
Hns. F
ff
Trpts. Bb
Trbns.
ff
Timp.
Tri.
S.D.
tr
p
f
Harp
Vlns. 1
Vlns. 2
Vlas.
'Cellos
Bass.

270

R
a2
Flts.
Obs.
Clts. A
Bsns.
ff
Hns. F
1 2
3 4
fp
Trpts. Bb
Trbns.
1 2
3
Timp.
Tri.
S.D.
Harp
Vlns. 1
arco
Vlns. 2
Vlas.
Cellos
Bass.

a2
Flts
ff
f
mf
Obs.
dim.
Clts. A
dim.
Bsns.
Hns. F
Trpts. Bb
Trbns.
Timp.
Tri.
dim
S.D
Harp
dim.
Vlns. 1
brillante
dim.
Vlns. 2
brillante
Pizz
dim
Vlas.
arco
div.
brillante
Pizz.
(non div.)
dim.
Cellos
arco div.
Pizz.
(non div.)
dim.
Bass.
brillante
(Pizz.)
dim.

280

Flts.
Obs.
Clts. A
Bsns.
Hns. F
Trpts. Bb
Trbns.
Timp.
Tri.
S. D.
Harp
Vlns. 1
Vlns. 2
Vlas.
Cellos
Bass.
mp
mf
ff
f
tr
arco
div.

S
𝅗𝅥 = 160
Flts.
a2
ff con spirito
Obs.
Clts. A
Bsns.
Hns. F
1
2
3
4
Tpts. Bb
Trbns.
Timp.
f con spirito
Cymb.
S.D.
f con spirito
Harp
fff
S
con spirito
𝅗𝅥 = 160
Vlns. 1
fff
con ff spirito
Vlns. 2
Vlas.
non-div.
div.
non div.
con ff spirito [ben marc.]
'Cellos
arco
div.
Bass.
con ff spirito [ben marc.]

Flts.
a2
Obs.
Clts. A
Bsns.
Hns. F
Solo
Tpts. Bb
Tbns.
Timp.
Cymb.
cl.
S. D.
Harp
Vlns. 1
Vlns. 2
Vlas.
div.
non-div.
soli
'Cellos
Bass.

280

Piccolo
Flts.
2° to Piccolo
Obs.
Clts. A
Bsns.
ff
Hns. F
marc.
marc.
Tpts. Bb
marc.
Tbns.
marc.
marc.
Timp.
Cymb.
cl.
Triangle
f
Harp
Vlns. 1
Vlns. 2
Vlas.
'Cellos
div.
non div.
Bass.
Pizz.
marc.

T
Pochiss. più mosso
Picc.
Fl. 1
Obs.
Clts. A
Bsns.
Hns. F
Trpts. Bb
Trbns.
Timp.
Cymb.
Tri.
Harp
Vlns. 1
Vlns. 2
Vlas.
'Cellos
Bass.
brillante
Pizz.
div.
unis.
(non div.)

290
Picc.
Fl. 1
Obs.
Clts. A
Bsns.
Hns. F
Tpts. Bb
Trbns.
Timp.
(cl.)
Cymb.
Glock.
ff
Harp
Vlns. 1
Vlns. 2
Vlas.
div.
'Cellos
Bass.

Tempo Giùsto

300

Poco più mosso

U Poco stringendo
Vlns. 1
Vlns. 2
Vlas.
Cellos
Bass.
Timp.
Glock.
tr
(cl.)
unis.

Printed and bound in Great Britain by
Caligraving Limited Thetford Norfolk

OXFORD UNIVERSITY PRESS